In **What A Time To Be Alone,** the Slumflower will be your life guru, confidante and best friend. She'll show you that being alone is not just okay: it's just about the best freaking thing that's ever happened to you. As she says, 'You're bad as hell and you were made with intention.' It's about time you realised.

Peppered with insightful Igbo proverbs from Chidera's Nigerian mother and full of her own original artwork, **What A Time To Be Alone** will help you navigate the modern world. Decide your self-worth, take time to heal and empower yourself in this messy world. Avoid other people's demons and realize that everyone is protecting themselves from something – no matter how aggressive their method. Sustain and grow healthy relationships and avoid toxicity in your friendships.

**Own your story. Create your own narrative.
Read this book.**

#WATTBA

'

WHAT A TIME TO BE ALONE

CHIDERA EGGERUE

Hardie Grant

QUADRILLE

Publishing Director Sarah Lavelle
Editor Susannah Otter
Designer Claire Rochford
Production Director Vincent Smith
Production Controller Tom Moore

Published in 2018 by Quadrille, an imprint
of Hardie Grant Publishing

Quadrille
52–54 Southwark Street
London SE1 1UN
quadrille.com

Cataloguing in Publication Data: a catalogue record
for this book is available from the British Library.

text and artwork © Chidera Eggerue 2018
design © Quadrille 2018

Reprinted in 2018 (three times), 2019
10 9 8 7 6 5

ISBN 978 1 78713 211 5

Printed in China

To my Mum, **who effortlessly yet intentionally led me to myself.**

What A Time To Be Alone is a book by a recovering hypocrite. It's here to remind you that no matter where you find yourself in life, you will ALWAYS have to face your truth. All of it. You're not alone, you're not crazy. Your feelings are valid and it's time to make peace with them... all of them.

This book has been divided into three important sections:

YOU.

is all about evaluating your self-worth, taking your time to heal and knowing how to handle yourself better in this messy world.

them.

is less about you and more about the ways other people can become dangerous if we don't know how to avoid their demons, but also about understanding that everybody is protecting themselves from something - no matter how aggressive their method is.

US

It's time we learn to find security in our solitude. Thankfully, it's never too late to find safety in yourself.

Are you ready to meet yourself?

 allows you to understand how to avoid toxicity, shows ways to grow and sustain productive relationships, and lists the healthiest ways to end relationships which no longer feel fruitful.

YOU.
YOU.
YOU.
YOU.
YOU.

YOU.
YOU.
YOU.
YOU.
YOU.

YOU ARE SUPPOSED TO BE HERE.

You might be lost, you might be confused, your life might feel like it lacks meaning, but you're still purposeful. Maybe you aren't doing as well as you thought you'd be doing by now, everyone around you looks like they've found their mojo, the world seems to be moving faster and further without you ... but just remember, you're still purposeful.

Loads of people (including yourself) find you annoying, you have an extreme case of butter fingers when it comes to handling important things like relationships and the lens you borrowed from your mate, people talk over you in group conversations but you're still purposeful.

Hope is never all lost. Hope is simply hiding and if you're reading this book, you're ready to find it!

FIRST THINGS FIRST:

Allowing other people to be time-killers while running away from the responsibility of loving ourselves happens to everyone, but it should be avoided. It always ends in emotional disaster. Nobody is ever going to be able to fill your you-shaped hole for you. No, not that hole. The gaping hole we all have inside that deeply craves validation, love and comfort. It just won't work. You've got to be fond of yourself enough to support yourself emotionally regardless of the intimate company of someone else. Loving yourself does not make you vain or conceited as long as you have respect for other people. The world loves to paint confidence in a terrible light because to be confident means to be self-sufficient. This is a threat to a world built on a multi-billion-dollar industry that tells you that you aren't doing you 'right'. Find your own sense of this, and the rest will follow.

SAVE SOME LOVE FOR YOURSELF.

YOU DESERVE IT.

TRY NOT TO BE A PRICK.

Human beings have been designed to disappoint. That's the brutal, sad reality. It's a pretty bitter, large pill to swallow, but once you finally come to terms with this truth, life won't hit you as hard anymore.

The thing about human beings is that we treat others the way we feel about ourselves, and most of the time, we don't even realise it. This is why it's important for you to learn to not internalise the way people choose to treat you. If, like me, you're one of those SUPER-SENSITIVE people who genuinely dies a little more inside every time someone takes advantage of your kindness, or pretty much ignores your existence whenever they feel like it, you've got to remind yourself that nothing is ever really that personal – even kindness. It's all a reflection of how that person is feeling about their self. So if someone decides to be a prick to you, don't bother yourself with the emotional turmoil. Just remember that they're fighting an even bigger battle with their self.

If in doubt, it's always wise to remind yourself that nobody who truly loves their self allows themselves to project negativity onto another human being. It does not get any more simple than this, my friend.

Having said that, we all carry the tendency to be pricks from time to time, especially to people we love. Over-comfort creates room for us to take people for granted. Remind people you love them more often. And try to remember their allergies.

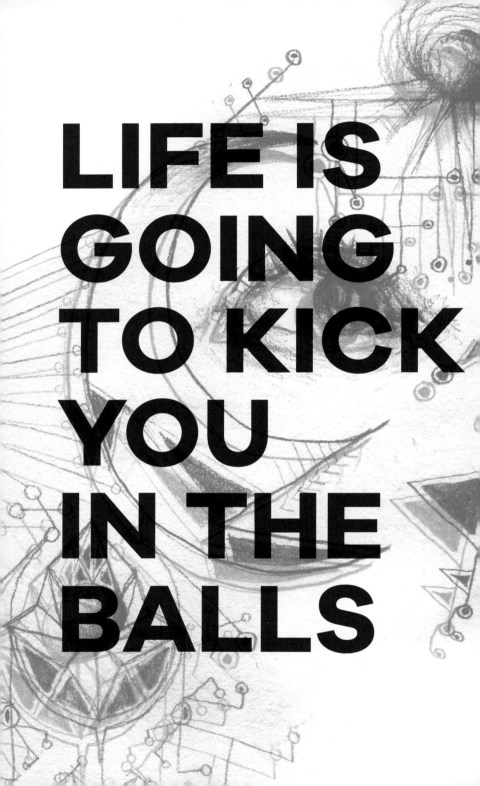

FOR
NO
REASON.

And the key is how you deal with it.
It's easier to blame yourself than
it is to accept that sometimes life
just needs to go wrong now for
things to go well later.

Healing hurts. Being kicked in the balls hurts. Being ignored hurts. Sometimes everything just hurts and you don't know why. As kids, we were always taught: if you want the wound to heal, don't touch it! Why? Because as good as it feels to scratch that painfully itchy scab, as good as it feels to ask that question you know you won't like the answer to, it only prolongs the healing process because you're shifting the scab out of place. Apply this to recovery from a traumatic event and notice the similarities in the damage done each time you revisit a scenario you wish you had had control over, then proceed to blame yourself for being 'stupid'. It hurts, doesn't it? You reach a point where you don't even know what hurts more: the trauma or your disappointment in yourself. The thing about healing is, it's a process. There will be times where you'll self-loathe, there will be times where you'll be so over it and there will even be times where you'll be sat for ages psychoanalysing every possible micro-event that led up to the event itself. You aren't crazy. You're human. Analysis, regression and regret are just as important as acceptance, forgiveness and forgetting. Every stage of the process, no matter how painful, matters. But if you really do want to grow past the pain, stop picking at the wound and just trust that it WILL heal one day. Everything you feel, no matter how deep or shallow, is temporary. If you ever catch yourself slipping back into despair, remind yourself of what Alan Watts says:

'Muddy water is best cleared by leaving it alone.'

DON'T FOCUS ON TRYING TO BE 'THE BEST'.

FOCUS ON BEING IRREPLACEABLE.

ONYE SỊ A CHA YA ISHI A CHARA JOHN? Ọ KWAKWARA ỊSHỊ JOHN KWARA?

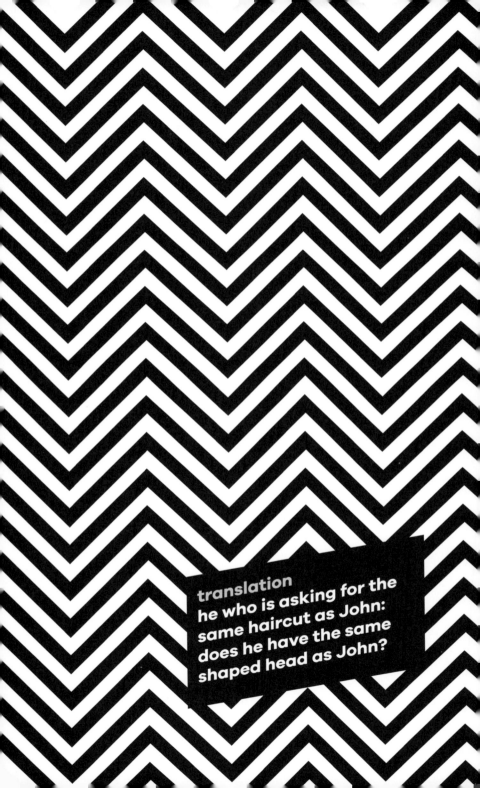

translation

he who is asking for the same haircut as John: does he have the same shaped head as John?

Being an Igbo Nigerian girl who grew up with Igbo as my first language, I have been raised on Nigerian proverbs and idioms that have literally saved my life. This proverb of having the same head shape as John is one that my mother often uses in 'biting off more than you can chew' or failing to 'cut your coat according to your size' scenarios. If we refuse to live according to what we have been presented with, we will only be met with disappointment which we have to face on our own. The only way to avoid disappintment is to be content with the present.

We often find ourselves comparing aspects of our lives to other people's. Social media hasn't helped one bit. With the rise of people creating online profiles, there's a whole new heap of added pressure to 'look like your life is together'. It's very easy to forget that social media allows you to literally present the life you wish you had to people you wish respected you a little more.

The problem with this is that people often make decisions based on the outcomes they've seen other people experience, expecting to see the same occur in their lives but the thing about life is: copying someone else's process won't necessarily get you their results. Looking like someone else won't give you the feeling you think they have of themselves.

Hanging out with people who you think 'look cool' won't necessarily make you cool if you are doing nothing to develop yourself to a level where you can be cool with you, without any other association with anybody. As long as you are not making the effort to create the life you want, your haircut is not going to look like John's, I'm afraid.

The time spent looking at other people is the time that should actually be spent on self-development. With all the time we spend 'preeing' other people's social-media accounts, imagine what we could have achieved by now if we directed all that energy inwards instead?

BOREDOM IS THE IDEAL BREEDING GROUND FOR BAD DECISIONS.

A lot of regrettable scenarios can be avoided if you just buckle down, focus on your goals and try not to give in to temporary temptations that will only distract and delay you from achieving the things you deserve. The biggest mistake you can make is to allow yourself to get sidetracked by people who will never be willing to stay with you during the storm they create in your life through their own selfishness.

DO BETTER.

'IT' DOESN'T REALLY GET BETTER.

YOU DO.

At some point, you finally 'get over it'. All of it. It stops keeping you awake at night. It stops giving you panic attacks. It stops reminding you of how out of control you really are of the world around you. Instead, getting over it reminds you of how in control you are of how you choose to interpret your experiences. It also reminds you that change will only ever create one thing: more change. So it's time we stopped fearing it and started being open to it. The fear of change is what delays growth. Sometimes, bad stuff needs to 'happen' to us in order for us to be equipped with one more nugget of wisdom which can end up being the most priceless thing you can discover by yourself. Bad stuff is going to keep happening because everything about life revolves around balance, so the best we can do for ourselves is to constantly carry the mindset that no pain ever goes to waste if you let it teach you.

if **love** doesn't teach you, **loss** will.

Beautiful things land in our lives whether we are ready to receive them or not. Love never seeks permission. Love just turns up unannounced. And if you fail to welcome it with warm arms and an open heart, prepare yourself for a lesson from the greatest teacher of all:

regret.

DO NOT CREATE EXPECTATIONS YOU KNOW YOU CANNOT LIVE UP TO.

QUIT OVER-EXPLAINING.

THE WORLD IS STILL GOING TO JUDGE YOU.

I still find myself trying really hard to be easy to digest and understand, but in doing that, I find that I keep compromising on WHO I AM. People still find a way to judge me regardless, so I have made it my aim to stop trying to be likeable and instead, just focus on being honest. When you die, nobody is going to remember you as the person who made sure they pleased everyone and silenced their self. The world does not care. We are all going to die. You do not exist to meet somebody else's standards. The only standards worth meeting are your own.

Stop waiting for people to give you permission to believe that you are amazing.

You don't need to change; just rearrange your priorities.

NGWERE SHỊ NA ELU ORJỊ DA SỊ NA YA GA ETO ONWEYE MA ỌWỤRỤ NA ONWEHỤ ỌNYE TORO YA.

It's important to keep in mind that the expectations of others only breed disappointment. If you learn to expect better from only yourself, you can become the architect of your joy. If we spend our lives waiting for people to tell us how proud of us they are, we will live in disappointment and die unhappy. But if we spend our lives recognising our own mini milestones and reminding ourselves of how far we've managed to come alone, we will live fulfilled and die content.

No matter how tiny or irrelevant you think your achievements are, you owe yourself that recognition. Your body has worked so hard to keep you alive long enough to be reading this sentence. It deserves a pat on the back from you.

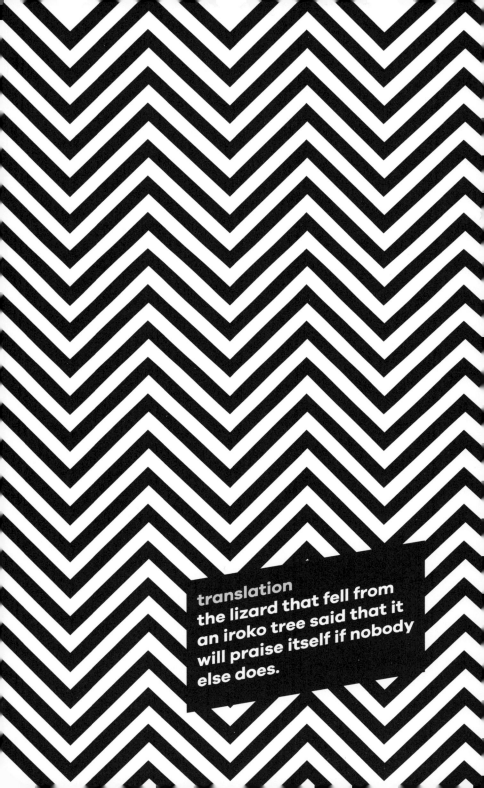

translation
the lizard that fell from
an iroko tree said that it
will praise itself if nobody
else does.

don't worry about how you're going to do it.

JUST DO

The scariest part of the process is starting. Starting is scary because it's new. And anything new comes with a set of possibilities. Possibilities scare us because there will always be outcomes we can't control. But part of setting healthy expectations for yourself is to focus on what you can control.

Back when I was a final-year university student, I used to constantly tell my dad that I truly had NO IDEA what I intended to do with myself after I graduated. Funny thing about that is that I ended up failing university. Great stuff. But anytime I expressed concerns like 'I've never had a job before in my life so how am I going to find a job that pays well and that I actually enjoy?' or 'I don't know what to do when I finish uni because I don't know how long I'll be job-seeking for and my student loan has run out so I'm not going to be able to afford to be jobless', he would just say to me:

'Finish being where you are first. It will all make sense later.'

IT FIRST.

ONYE AKWỌ NA AZU AMAHU NA IJE NA ARA AHỤ.

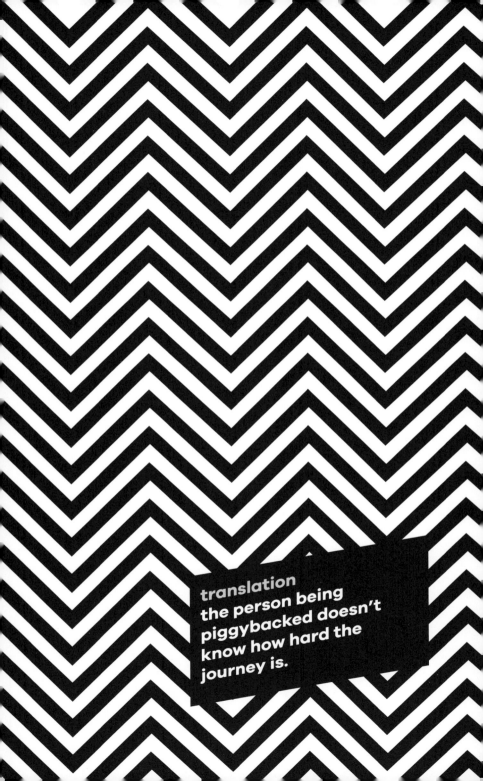

translation
the person being piggybacked doesn't know how hard the journey is.

Recognise your privilege! Whiteness is a privilege; being 'pretty' is a privilege; being born in a country that isn't war-torn is a privilege. Being born white means you'll be treated 'better' than a person of colour in some way or another – be it subtle or obvious. Being seen as pretty according to society's standards means you'll receive 'better' attention than someone who does not fit the standards. Being born in a country that isn't war-torn means you'll have a 'better' chance of having a higher life expectancy than someone who doesn't have this privilege.

But privilege is not necessarily a bad thing – it's how you treat others based on it, it's how you use it to shape your own life, it's how you allow it to influence the way you view yourself that matters. The thing about privilege is that it's not a right. Unless you are made to understand that privilege doesn't automatically make you more deserving of good things than another human being, you will roam this world being self-entitled. Let's take whiteness as an example. White people are not born bad. Your race does not define the quality of your character. However, the <u>learned</u> self-entitlement that often comes with whiteness creates a way of thinking that breeds the mentality that whiteness has more value than blackness and, for this reason, the world is in a situation where a black person is seen as 'less valuable' than a white person. But there are ways around navigating white privilege:

As a white person, make room to listen to the experiences of people who do not have your privilege. Do not speak over them. Do not tell them how to deal with an experience you literally know nothing of - if a strawberry is complaining about losing seeds and you are a lemon, it is not your place to tell the strawberry how to deal with their seed loss, is it? If you are called out on your privilege and you feel attacked, you have the right to defend yourself when appropriate, but please, do not weaponise your tears in order to gain sympathy and make yourself the centre of the narrative. Because of the way society views whiteness as fragile, delicate and pure, there's nothing more 'powerful' than the tears of a white woman when she's in the same space as a black woman. If a white woman is seen crying in a situation involving a black woman, no matter the narrative, the black woman is automatically viewed as the monster and the white woman is viewed as the victim. This is exactly how white privilege works.

We are living in a society where whiteness is piggybacking off blackness – colonised land, misappropriated culture, stolen artefacts in museums ... The list continues to grow. Yet the moment a black person complains that their back is getting tired, they are silenced and told 'it can't be that heavy'; 'slavery ended ages ago, get over it'; 'let's move forward and stop focusing on the past'.

The four-year-old you. Depleted self esteem can get in the way of your goals. Anytime you find yourself in an environment that dilutes your self-esteem, picture four-year-old you and try your best to be her hero.

When you're about to tell yourself that you're ugly and not good enough, visualise yourself saying all those things to four-year-old you. How does it feel to be verbally abusive to a four-year-old? How does it feel to be that four-year-old being verbally abused by the one person she needs the most?

The only difference between four-year-old you and current you is time. You're still the same fragile human being who wants to be loved. You're still the same fragile human being who wants to be told, 'Wow, you're so amazing. Well done!' You're still the same fragile human being who simply wants to be held.

Imagine a little four-year-old you taking ages creating a really amazing gift for someone really special to you, only to be ignored when you present it ...

I bet 'grown-up' you still goes through that, don't you? This is the same as current you going out of your way to share yourself with people who don't want to make room for you. You reshape yourself for them but it's never enough. You repeat your jokes but they never laugh. You reduce your voice so you don't 'complain too much'. By the time you realise you're doing all this, they've probably already ditched you for someone who interests them more.

Even if you don't think current you is deserving of love, do it for four-year-old you.

The fixer.
You try to be 'hotter'. You try to complain less. You change your perfume. You wear 'nicer' clothes. You stop being 'too confident'. You shrink yourself. It hurts a lot but you continue doing it because you need the approval. You need the validation. You're scared to move on because 'nobody else can replicate this bond'. Because 'we go way back'. Because you think you can 'fix' this. You think you created this problem. But the problem was never you. Stop falling in love with empty people and trying to fill them with you.

You'll lose, each and every time.

The fixer.

DON'T LET YOUR KINDNESS KILL YOU.

Let's face it: fixers like you and I are people who wish we had a little more control over our lives, so we vicariously live through the process of attempting to fix other people.

You have a saviour complex! There are no rewards for this. When you have a saviour complex, it's often difficult to distinguish between whether you are a necessity to someone or merely an accessory to them.

People with a saviour complex often have abandonment issues and try to make themselves indispensable and irreplaceable to people by turning themselves into an emotional toolbox.

Trying to make yourself overtly 'useful' in other people's lives without observing how much they even value your effort can be a prevention mechanism used to try and overpower your abandonment issues.

I've learnt to hold my importance in other people's lives to a default setting of neutral, which allows me to manage my own abandonment issues without projecting any inflated expectations on others.

Sometimes, fixing looks like shrinking. You make yourself smaller to give the other person more room to grow. Other times, fixing looks like fighting. You try the tough love approach but it's only met with friction, which becomes distance, which eventually morphs into apathy. No matter how pure your intentions are, you cannot make someone meet their self. Your kindness gets taken the wrong way when you think you're helping, but don't realise that you are actually causing damage.

Minding your business is the new black. Try it. I'm sure we can all remember a situation where we thought we were doing good, only for the person we were doing it for to turn around and attack us. If you ever find yourself in a scenario where your kindness gets you in trouble, redirect that energy to yourself. You need you more than anybody else could ever need you.

SILENCE CAN NEVER BE MISQUOTED.
That's one more quote from my brilliant mother. She's such a G, right? Listen to your elders, because most of the time, they're right. My mother always says to me: 'What I can see sitting down, you can't even see standing up!' See? She's right.

She also taught me that your mouth can either save you or get you killed, so if in doubt, shut your mouth. She does have a point; the less you say, the less you can be held for. Learning to mind your business is a skill that cannot be taught. It is something you have to be willing to learn from life itself.

We have all been in situations where we have gone a step too far and said way more than necessary, which has eventually landed us in trouble. I've learnt from experience that if the situation does not directly concern you or someone you cannot live without, tune out, because when it goes it goes tits up, all the pitchforks will be coming in your direction. Laying low and focusing on your own problems is the key.

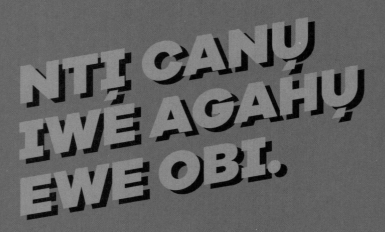

NTỊ CANỤ IWÉ AGAHỤ EWE OBI.

Sometimes, it's better to just not 'know'. I've learnt to avoid asking questions I know I might not like the answer to. This is one of those rare times in life where ambiguity should be met with silence. Preservation of your mental health is one of the most important things you can do for yourself. It's tempting to go through your partner's phone. It's tempting to go to their profile to see what they're indirectly saying about you. Handing over your power often occurs in the form of ruffling the silence. But one thing I've learnt from my mother is this: where there's peace, allow it to reign.

translation
if the ear doesn't hear,
the heart will not be
upset.

THE SOONER WE STOP PRETENDING TO BE IMMUNE TO FEELINGS THAT SCARE US, THE SOONER LIFE WILL BEGIN TO MAKE SENSE.

You run because it feels scary to care this much.

You run because you associate loving with losing. You run because facing these feelings raises the responsibility of facing up to yourself.

To care is to be vulnerable. According to the world, it's not cool to be vulnerable; it's cool to be stoic, aloof and unconcerned, because to emotionally inept people, this shows resilience, strength of character and the oh-so-admirable quality of being eternally unbothered. But this is all wrong, because to be constantly 'unbothered' is to be dead inside. For a lot of people, caring means losing. These are the people who invest all their energy into performing instead of living, because to appear unbothered all the time, you must be in a constant state of pretence. Don't aim to be like these people. They need more help than you think you do. But it is not your place to save them.

I've stopped being disappointed in the way people have chosen to treat me. It's often a reflection of their relationship with their self. Nothing lasts when you aren't content with your being. Nothing. Once you reach a point where you stop feeling like a victim and more like a student of life, your life becomes more meaningful. You need YOU more than you need anyone else. Sympathy feels really good when you're caught up in self-destruction, but anytime I find myself slipping into my toxic victim mentality, I remind myself:

Whatever happens to me, I'm in control.

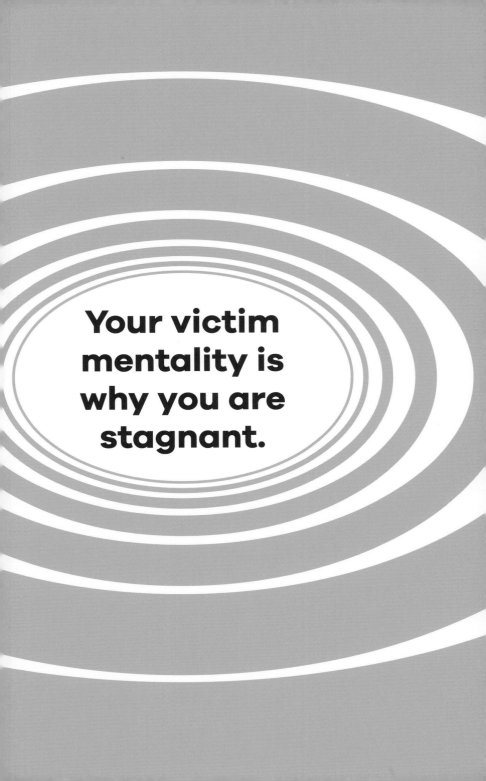

Your victim mentality is why you are stagnant.

remember: never feel defeated by a 'no'.

take it as a

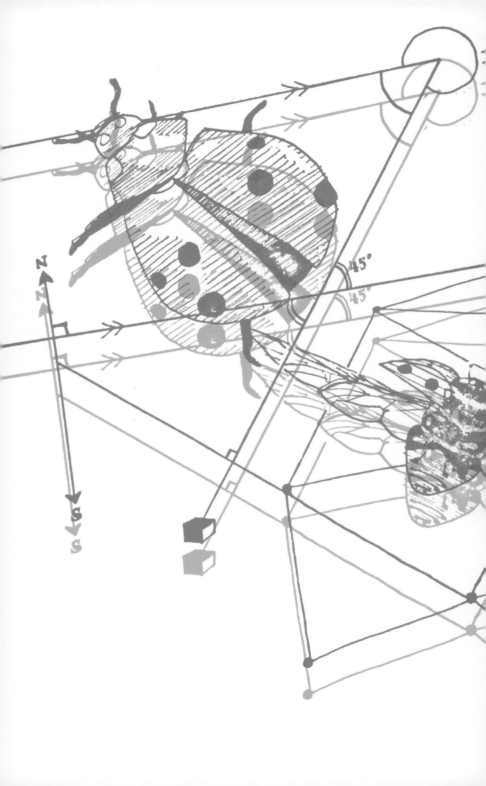

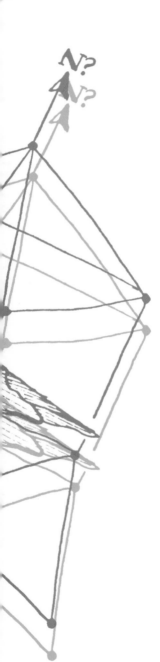

LEARN TO 'TAKE ANY LOSS LIKE A BOSS'

No matter how much it hurts, no matter how embarrassing it feels. Grow through it. Let it teach you. Every situation that does not work in our favour is there to show us a side of us that we really needed to see. If you aren't losing, you aren't learning.

Everything happening to you, is for you. Life is one big cosmic mess but everything you're going through is pushing you closer to the person you need to be. Human beings are finding smarter ways to curate the lives they wish they had for other people to observe them through a phone screen. But they don't tell you that the better your life gets, the bigger your demons become. Just remember that everything revolves around balance. It will never be perfect but it will always get better. When it gets unbearable, it's worth remembering: these are the problems that you didn't know you asked for when you were praying for those blessings.

Tasting your own magic

Be nice to yourself. Go to Nando's alone. Take walks along the river on your own. Have super-long baths and blast your favourite playlist whilst you do so. Stop waiting for someone to give you that unconditional fairytale love and give it to yourself. Start right now. Unfollow people who give you weird energy. Mute and block people who make you feel uncomfortable for whatever reason. Protect your space and pay no mind to how people may perceive you doing this. You deserve greatness, so give it to yourself. We need to learn to stop feeling so guilty for being kind to ourselves. If you sit around waiting for someone to come and rescue you from yourself, life will pass you by – it ain't gon' happen.

MAMỊ RỊ
ARAHỤ ÁHỤ
MANA
OKỤKỌ
AGÁHỤ
ANYỤLỊ YE.

translation
to pee is not hard but a
chicken can never do it.

**You ever seen a chicken pee?
Of course not!
Chickens don't pee.**

They do release waste but you'll never see a stream of urine leave a chicken's body. You might be wondering why you're reading about chickens peeing; peeing is so ordinary – why is peeing such a big deal? You're right. Peeing is not a big deal to us. But to a chicken, it's an unfathomable task.

We spend so much time dwelling on goals we haven't achieved and dreams we think we can't reach that we forget to actually realise how magical we are as human beings. The ability to pee is a blessing in itself. It means your body is working; it means you are healthy; it means you are alive. Peeing is so effortless to us but we never stop to actually think about the complexity of the process our bodies undergo just to create pee. We take our cells for granted. We take ourselves for granted. We fail to recognise how powerful we are as human beings.

Next time you go for a pee, think about how complex, special and magical you are.

Repeat after me:

I do not owe anybody 'pretty'. Whichever state I choose to show up in will always be enough.
I do not owe anybody 'pretty'. Whichever state I choose to show up in will always be enough.
I do not owe anybody 'pretty'. Whichever state I choose to show up in will always be enough.
I do not owe anybody 'pretty'. Whichever state I choose to show up in will always be enough.
I do not owe anybody 'pretty'. Whichever state I choose to show up in will always be enough.

You are not here for anybody's consumption or amusement.

DO YOU KNOW HOW SHORT LIFE IS?

Too short to be convincing other
people that you are worthy.

Choose yourself.

Over and over again.

Even when you've let yourself down.

Choose yourself.

Even when it feels uncomfortable.

Choose yourself.

Even when you're tired.

Choose yourself.

SELF-LOVE IS THE LEAST AGGRESSIVE, MOST EFFECTIVE, FORM OF INTIMIDATION.

You cannot deceive someone who knows what they want. You cannot control someone who knows who they are.

Because it is controlled by tiny insecure people with large estates, the world wants us to shrink ourselves.

Here are three mantras to read to yourself when the feelings of inadequacy start creeping in:

1. For the world, I'll always be too much of one thing or not enough of another, but for myself I will ALWAYS be enough.

2. No matter how much time I choose to spend with myself, none of it is ever wasted. I am a lifetime investment and I am worth the wait.

3. Once I learn to own my space, I will never be afraid of deciding who deserves access to it. I am a special person and I deserve the same respect that I go out of my way to give others.

them.
them.
them.
them.
them.

them.
them.
them.
them.
them.

NO MATTER WHAT, ALWAYS REMEMBER: YOU ARE ALLOWED TO CHANGE YOUR MIND ABOUT HOW YOU FEEL ABOUT OTHER PEOPLE.

If they keep bringing up your past, they belong in it.
We reject the truth that people treat you not how they feel about you but how they feel about themselves. This is because the ego wants to be centre of attention at all times. When things go wrong with other people, it's easier for you to blame yourself than it is to accept that sometimes people don't know how to act when they have nice things simply because they have never had nice things. It's not your responsibility to make anybody like their life.

Sometimes, people don't like their lives but that's not supposed to be your problem. When people dislike themselves, they tend to make poor decisions. You know people's poor decisions are in no way reflective of your value, right?

We need to stop feeling bad for protecting ourselves from people who do not put our best interests first. Communicate exactly how you are feeling without worrying about scaring people away. If asserting your boundaries scares people, they don't deserve you. Tell people you're drained so that they stop using your mind to alleviate themselves of their own responsibility for their own poor decisions.

You can't have peace if you're overthinking other people's choices ... if they cared, they'd be careful.

I wish there was a way to take back familiarity. Certain people just don't deserve to know you like that. Your feelings matter, no matter how bitter you look to other people. In regards to validating your own feelings: if you feel used, you have been used. Your intuition can detect an imbalance way before your mind registers it. So if you feel like raising your standards for your own betterment, do so.

People hate seeing you raise your standards because it makes them question their own ability to raise their's. Feeling sad about your life and watching someone else live a better one should teach you that other people's better decisions can create resentment. People with low standards are always the first to tell you you're asking for too much.

Sometimes, people get a rush out of being mean to you because it's the closest they can get to reclaiming power over their own lives. When I say that nothing anybody ever does is ultimately because of you, this is exactly what I mean.

A lot of the time, people mask their care for you with insults because they feel out of control when they look at you, and the only way they can regain that control is to behave in a way that makes them feel powerful.

But what we have all yet to understand is that hurting someone else is still hurting yourself. You just feel the pain much later.

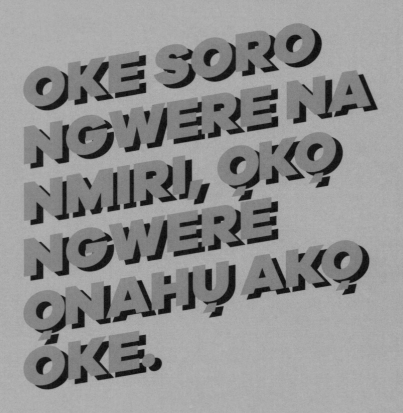

OKE SORO NGWERE NA NMIRI, ỌKỌ NGWERE ỌNAHỤ AKỌ ỌKE.

Mother always taught me: be careful who you blindly follow. Just because someone looks like you and appears to be similar to you, this does not mean you are built to survive in the same environment. Some people have pasts that have taught them how to adapt to certain scenarios life may present. Just because your homie popped a molly and enjoyed it, does not mean you will have the same reaction. You might hate it. *TRIGGER WARNING* You might even die.

This is not to say that trying new things is bad; this is just to say that not every rag needs to be wrung completely dry. Not everything needs to be tried, especially if your gut is telling you to leave it be. Fitting in is overrated.

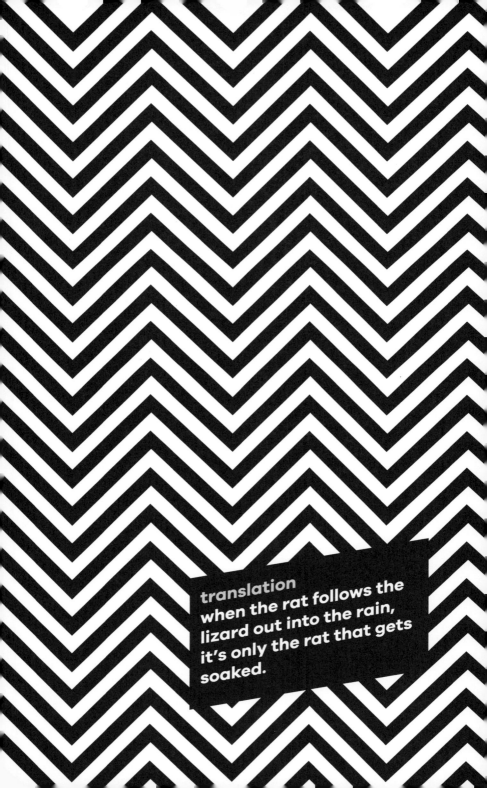

translation
when the rat follows the lizard out into the rain, it's only the rat that gets soaked.

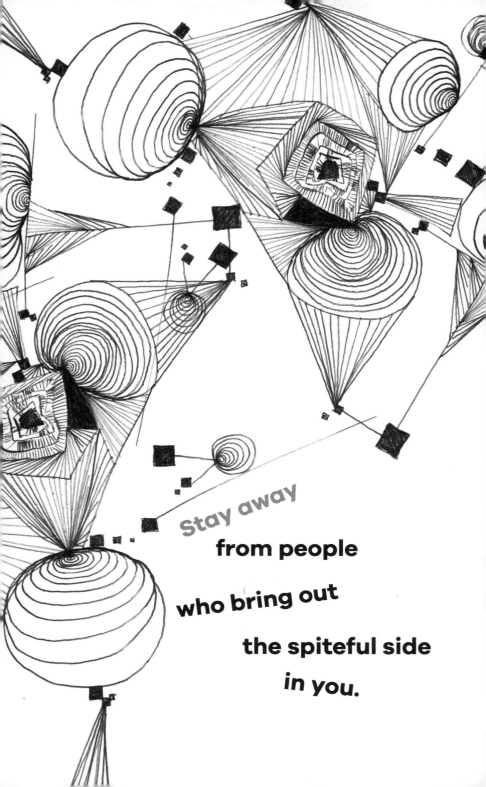

Stay away
from people
who bring out
the spiteful side
in you.

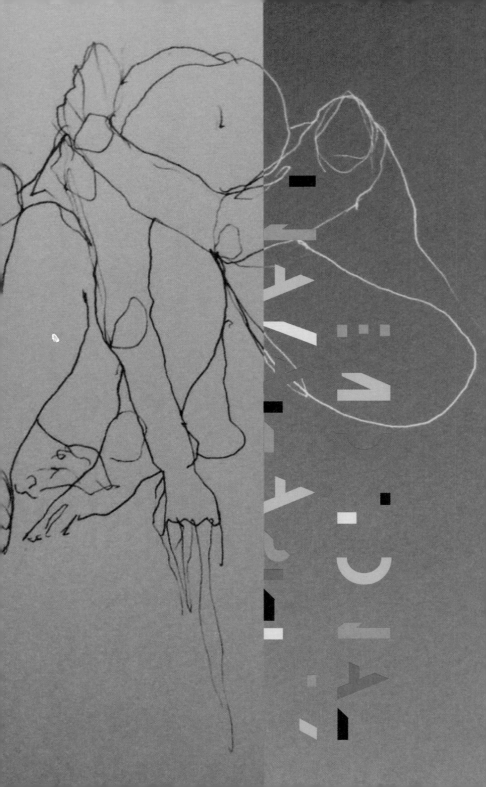

EMOTIONAL UNAVAILABILITY

Emotionally unavailable people always return when you cut them off because they want their control back. It's not you they want. It's flattering that they finally came back but proving this point can be very overrated when it comes to your mental well-being. When your kindness-abuser does make their much-anticipated and triumphant re-entry into your life, they will also make sure to position themselves in order to put YOU back in the position of vulnerability. Vulnerable people are easy to control.

An emotionally unavailable person can never truly value you. They are only around you because they value the validation you give them. Remember that emotionally unavailable people are scared of their own feelings. That's why they're never able to properly interact with yours either. They either dismiss them or dilute them.

You have to understand that behind every emotionally unavailable individual you interact intimately with is a terrified person who is afraid of losing their power to you (remember: they often associate loving with losing). Ever noticed how much they enjoy ignoring your texts, tweets or even emails? And that when you pull them up on it, they make you feel like such a stalker? This is because they receive ego strokes from ignoring you. Their ignoring of you only makes you work harder for their validation. This makes them treat you worse. But it's never too late to reclaim your power.

To hit an emotionally unavailable person where it hurts, cut them off and restrict them from access to your thoughts. Block them on as many of your social media accounts as you can. Take charge of your space. Switch the power dynamic.

This works because blocking this person forces them out of their position of control. How? They now don't know what you are thinking, doing or feeling. But in order for them to protect their ego, they will tell their self that you blocking them means they have 'won', because to people like this, EVERYTHING is about power and everything is a game. They are also the type to never compliment you about anything because they don't want you to know how great you are. If you know, you'll leave.

If they're the type to complain about people being 'too emotional', they're emotionally unavailable. No self-aware, mature human being stigmatises others for having feelings. Empathy is often what emotionally unavailable people lack. This is the reason why they will most likely never change: they place all their value in their egos. Until a person is able to love their self enough to make peace with their ego, they will never experience the full spectrum of happiness that comes with being with someone else. A lot of the time, if you're close to someone (close enough to be concerned about how you're being treated) but they resist revealing their vulnerability to you, it is because they are terrified and are masking this fear with their pride – which to them, is more important than forming a proper bond with you. Again, they just want to use you for an ego boost.

Think about it: you cannot form a solid bond without vulnerability. Vulnerability means putting your ego aside. This is their biggest fear. Have you noticed that emotionally unavailable people only conveniently appear when they want something from you, but are AWOL when you need them? They are the type to hide behind 'I'm busy' but they're never busy when they want to use you!

But the irony is that an emotionally unavailable person almost always becomes fonder of the person that leaves them, not the other way round. Because there's nobody more attractive than someone who loves their self enough to implement boundaries that exclude people who are toxic to them. The annoying thing about us human beings is that we are always subconsciously attracted to what we cannot have, even if we once had it.

This is why they always come back when you leave them: familiar territory, combined with their romanticised memories of you.

If a person is withholding vulnerablity from you, it can be because their pride is more important than forming a bond with you. Pride is the product of fear. The ego is terrified of being in a position of doubt. Pride offers protection. The ego sees vulnerability as a threat. But to love is to weaken the walls the ego has built and this is the ego's worst nightmare. If someone has more pride than vulnerability to show you, they are not in a position to love you healthily.

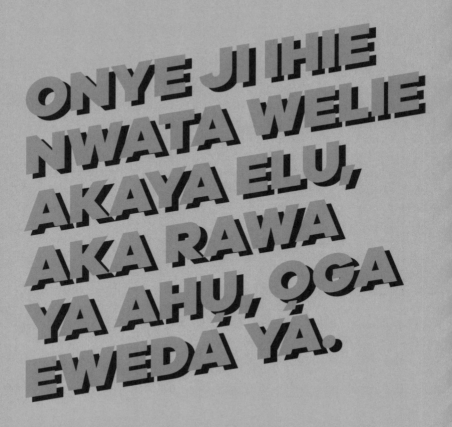

ONYE JI IHIE NWATA WELIE AKAYA ELU, AKA RAWA YA AHỤ, ỌGA EWEDA YA.

Bullies will always quit in the end. Insecure people receive a rush from getting a reaction out of someone they have a hold over. But they give up when they realise that their victim has grown indifferent to their abusive tactics.

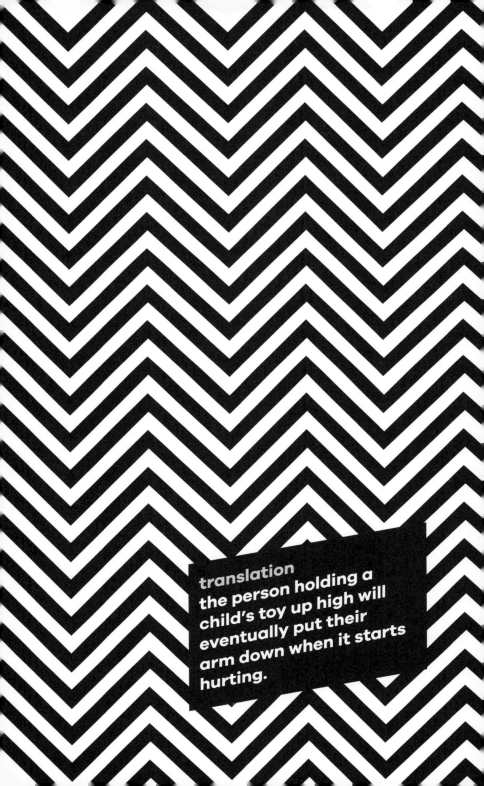

translation
the person holding a child's toy up high will eventually put their arm down when it starts hurting.

Never
give
people a
second
chance
to
violate
you ... no matter how
small-
or
large-scale
it was.

It doesn't matter how 'long ago' the violation was. As long as you feel as if that person doesn't deserve contact with you, stand firm – even if they try to gaslight you by calling you 'crazy'. This is the last flop a fish makes before it dies. It's always tempting to give them a third chance based on 'nice' behaviour, but their currently being nice to you doesn't cancel out the particular violation that still affects you.

Put your peace of mind first.

They don't even deserve an explanation as to why you don't want to speak to them again. An interaction with you is too much of a reward. With the level of self-love I've reached, certain people will never be hearing from me again – that would be far too much of a privilege.

MGBE NKITA HURU OZU ỌKỤKỌ...

My mother always says to me in Igbo: 'When the chicken saw the corpse of the dog, it's fine. But when the dog sees the corpse of the chicken, it's trouble for the dog.' Why? Everyone will instantly assume the dog killed the chicken.

There's this disease the world suffers from called racism. White people are the chicken and black people are the dog in this scenario. As black people, we are constantly having to tiptoe to avoid being caught in a dog & chicken situation. We can't be armed in a state that permits firearm bearing because we will always be seen as a threat. So we get shot dead on sight by police with no benefit of prior investigation.

But there have been identical scenarios where white people have been taken into custody alive and breathing after carrying out mass shootings because remember: it's okay for the chicken to see the dead body of the dog; there's no possible way the death could be the chicken's fault!

translation
when the dog sees the
corpse of the chicken...

friends who give you weird energy that you can't quite place your finger on

They flake on you when you make plans to meet up; either they 'forgot' or 'something came up last minute'. But this doesn't happen once; this happens enough for you to recognise a pattern that spells out 'I don't really care about you, I care about how you make me feel when I need to kill some time, but right now, I've found something more important to involve myself in, so I'll drop you and pick you up if/when I feel like, because I know you'll be there waiting on me'. People don't flake on what they believe is necessary. Even if something genuinely comes up, they will give you enough notice but also make an effort to rearrange to meet up and fully follow through with it. Not flake again. If you can relate to being on the receiving end of this, don't bother responding to that person anymore if your relationship with them can be minimised. You deserve to spend your time with people who value it. Remember: anybody who does not respect your time, does not respect you.

If you feel like you're a flake, quit it. A lot of the time, flakiness comes from heavy anxiety. As someone who has dealt with very serious anxiety, I'll let you know this: you're better off keeping your distance consistently, rather than flaking here and there and becoming known as an inconsistent person.

Ever been in a situation when someone you consider a close friend suddenly stops congratulating you on your achievements like real friends should? As much as external validation is not something we should be reliant on, it is important to keep in mind that someone who calls their self your friend is someone you should be able to share your joy with; someone who encourages you to go for it; someone who reminds you not to give up; someone who cheers you on. If you are beginning to notice that your friend no longer plays a supportive role in your life, it's important to understand where this sudden change of energy has come from. It's a tough one to admit to yourself, but they may simply be jealous of you, especially if you are always coming to them with good news. This can sometimes create jealousy because you are reminding them of what they wish they could achieve – especially if they are in a stagnant place in life.

But jealousy doesn't make you a bad person. Being a flake doesn't make you a bad person. These behaviours are all responses to deeper personal issues. While it's wise to minimise time spent with people who set off alarm bells in your gut, it's also compassionate to keep in the back of your mind that people are really out here trying to fight their demons.

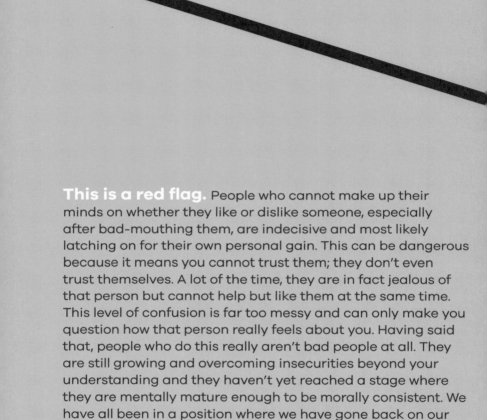

This is a red flag. People who cannot make up their minds on whether they like or dislike someone, especially after bad-mouthing them, are indecisive and most likely latching on for their own personal gain. This can be dangerous because it means you cannot trust them; they don't even trust themselves. A lot of the time, they are in fact jealous of that person but cannot help but like them at the same time. This level of confusion is far too messy and can only make you question how that person really feels about you. Having said that, people who do this really aren't bad people at all. They are still growing and overcoming insecurities beyond your understanding and they haven't yet reached a stage where they are mentally mature enough to be morally consistent. We have all been in a position where we have gone back on our word and behaved like a total hypocrite. This is part of being human but it isn't justifiable. We can all do better. If you feel like you are very similar to this type of behaviour, ask yourself these questions:

people who suddenly start hanging out with the same people they've been claiming to 'dislike'

What is it that draws me to this person that I dislike?

Why do I dislike them; is it because they remind me of myself?

Does this reminder threaten my sense of identity?

Does this person remind me of who I wish to be but I haven't figured out how to get there yet?

Am I taking my frustration at myself out on this person?

ONYE NA ERE IGBE OZU NA EKPE EKPERE ONWU NDE NMADU, MANA ONA-ATU UJO ONWU KARIA ONYE OBULA.

Horrible people, surprisingly, don't like it
when you're horrible to them.

translation
a coffin merchant prays
for the death of others
but fears death more
than anyone else.

SOMETIMES, 'I FORGOT' ACTUALLY MEANS 'I DIDN'T CARE ENOUGH TO PAY ATTENTION'.

Let's be real: this is subjective. But you'll know when someone you care about forgets something seemingly unforgettable. You'll know when someone you care about overlooks the significant details about you. You'll know when someone prefers the idea of you to the reality of you.

You'll know.

People know exactly what they're doing when they're taking advantage of you.

Apologies do not change intentions.

Not figuring out sooner doesn't make you stupid. Sadly, being a 'nice person' does not pay off if you don't know how to stand up for yourself and integrate more 'no' into your life. In fact, being a nice person is overrated. It doesn't make you a unicorn; it's just basic human etiquette. If people are wise enough to want you, they should be wise enough to treat you well, but they make the choice not to because, to selfish people, being kind drains them of their power.

But selfish people are so necessary. In fact, I'm so thankful for all the selfish people I've ever come across. They pushed me away so far that I had no choice but to face myself. I had to learn to stop feeling guilty for making people aware of how their selfish decisions directly affected me. Selfish people are placed in your life to remind you of the importance of loving yourself first.

IF YOU FEEL A WEIRD BIT OF GUILT/ DISCOMFORT AFTER SHARING GOOD NEWS,

YOU'RE SHARING YOURSELF WITH THE WRONG PERSON.

ONYE JI IHIE GỊ SORO GỊ NÁ ACHỌ YA, GAHỤ AHỤ YA.

Be mindful of who you take advice from. Manipulative people are skilled infiltrators of the mind.

translation
if someone is helping you
look for what they stole
from you, you'll never
find it.

Don't be scared to raise your standards! Nothing is ever worth lowering them for. Stand firm in what you believe you deserve. When you raise your **standards** for yourself, you stop getting excited over people showing interest in you because you're interested in you too!

Don't be afraid to raise your **standards**. You'd actually be surprised to know that there's someone out there more than willing to meet them. I used to be scared of having overly high **standards** until I met people who lived up to them without even trying. This is YOUR life and you are allowed to dictate your **standards** for yourself.

You become a lot more strict with your **standards** when you realise how valuable you are. You also learn to understand that you were carefully created with intention, purpose and a divine reason that exists beyond surface value and you do not have to meet anybody's **standards** if you do not want to.

Once you've managed to raise your **standards**, it's important to not let your boredom lower them. Boredom and loneliness creates the ideal breeding ground for bad decisions.

Another thing that happens when you raise your **standards** is that you'll be presented with people who regard breaching your boundaries as a challenge and will seek a thrill in attempting to find loopholes in your requirements. You're a human being. There will be times when you'll be tempted to lower your **standards**. There will be times when people will be worth the exception because the value they add to your life is meaningful to you.

What they don't tell you is that the higher your **standards** are, the stronger the temptation will be to compromise. Because having higher requirements for your life can be isolating. Not everybody feels the need to demand better for their lives. Having higher **standards** often means you'll no longer be able to relate as much (or at all) to the same people you used to enjoy spending time with. This is the bittersweet part of it all. But choosing yourself is never a bad idea. Prioritising your **standards** does not make you selfish.

It's hard to find a motivator to maintain your **standards** but sometimes, pain from the past can help you. I still have anger I've been holding onto for years, but as long as that anger doesn't warp the way I speak to and view myself, it's productive because it allows me to protect myself properly and use the pain as a reference each time I'm tempted to lower my **standards**!

Everytime you raise your **standards**, life sets you with a new challenge to confirm how seriously you take yourself. Our biggest challenges in life often occur in the form of dealing with other people. Keep an eye out for any behaviour that makes you double-take. It's always worth a second look.

NOT EVERY APOLOGY IS GENUINE.

Sometimes, people do not apologise to you so that they can rectify their wrongs and regain your trust. Sometimes, people apologise to rid themselves of their own guilt. Other times, people apologise to smooth the ground, which allows them to ask you for something in future or even use you for an undeserved favour. This ground is a grey area: it is a neutral. It will not benefit you, particularly if people are using it to ask you for favours.

Be attentive, as well, of how long it takes someone to apologise to you. A true friend who values their relationship with you will make the effort to recognise and accept their wrongs as soon as they can. A friend who never really cared about you to begin with will give you a very late apology, something along the lines of 'I'm so proud of you, I've seen your progress whils we haven't been speaking' – which is a bit of a red flag as they're most likely returning because they have seen that you're actually doing pretty well in life, contrary to their hopes.

With all that's been said, you will know when it feels genuine. You will. In-between fall-outs, life happens and time passing isn't always a good indication of how genuine someone is being, so always listen to your gut. The gut never lies.

NGE NWATA NA EBE AKWA NA-ATỤ AKA, IHIE NA EMEYA AKWA NỌ NGAHỤ.

That crying child is your intuition. Where there is smoke, there is fire. Ignoring your intuition is far too much of a risk. You'll start to listen to your intuition more when you get tired of that inner voice telling you 'I told you so'. The truth is, your life will slide back into alignment when you stop shouting over your intuition. It's time for less asking people for advice, time for more allowing yourself to be guided by your own intuition. Sometimes the crying child is your intuition pointing at a person who brings out a very unhealthy side of you. Sometimes, the people unhealthiest for us can also be the people we have the most fun with. Just because you're having fun, it doesn't mean you're using your time effectively – especially if you have time-specific goals you know you should be working on.

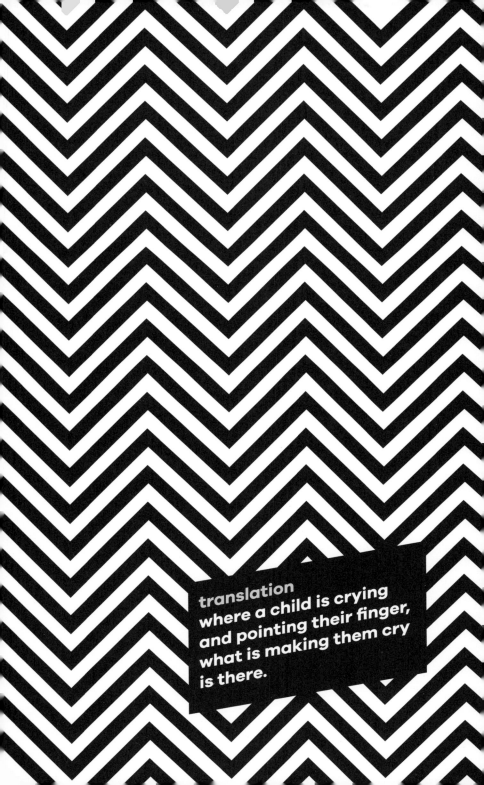

translation
where a child is crying
and pointing their finger,
what is making them cry
is there.

THE
FEAR
OF
OPENING
UP

The problem.
People can run away from us when they discover the dark past that has shaped the beautiful light that attracted them to us in the first place. It took a while for me to understand that people who run from things in you can, in fact, be running away from facing the same thing in themselves.

When you make the effort to learn to understand yourself, this makes it a lot easier for you to understand other people.

People who run away from themselves can run away from other people in the most subtle to the most extreme ways. You may have experienced people who crash into your life like a wave then suddenly disappear like a retreating tide.

It's the most draining thing to be fond of someone who is only fond of you when they're bored. But one thing that's important to keep in mind is that you shouldn't cling onto how nice they selectively are to you as a justification of why you should allow them to continue treating your life like a hostel.

The solution.
Observe the fact that they repeatedly make the choice to flake/disappear on you with no remorse. Anybody who does not respect your time does not respect you.

It can be terrifying to ever open up again to someone after you've experienced rejection of who you are in the past. But the trick is to share yourself in ever so tiny pieces so that you can gauge how much the person you are sharing yourself with respects your story.

Sometimes, people just don't deserve to know us like that.

YOU CANNOT SAVE ANYONE.

Scenario: So you've met this fine piece of wonderful human who you've totally convinced yourself that you're smitten with.

● ● ●

But: they smoke cigarettes and you despise someone you 'love' smoking because it's slow suicide (like most pleasures in this world, to be honest). You try to convince them to stop smoking for their own good (even though deep down in the hidden corridors of your intentions you want them to do it for you; to prove their love for you).

Each time you see them light up another cigarette, you find a new passive-aggressive, emotionally-driven way to remind them that smoking is bad for them, and they respond with a passive aggressive remark that makes you feel bad for nagging them about their addiction. The scenario repeats itself until you finally give up and implement the whole 'Fine, I'll accept you for who you are then' approach where you just don't say anything else because, at this point, you've finally learnt that you cannot force someone to change for your sake if they aren't even willing to change for their own self.

Moral of the scenario: If you know you cannot live with someone you've chosen to love living a lifestyle you don't agree with, you have the choice to either accept them as they are from the beginning or leave them to be with someone who accepts them.

Trying to change someone else will only change **YOU**.

There's always a reason why someone is the way that they are.

The reason might not always be one that you will like or understand, but the sooner you make peace with it, the sooner you will have peace. Trying to shake someone out of who they have been their entire life is like trying to reverse the flow of water in a tap. It just will not happen. People will remain in their ways until life gives them a reason to stop, think and change for THEIR OWN betterment. Some people do not ever change. Because they are so used to their problems, that they prefer familiar struggles to the struggles of growing out of being a problematic person.

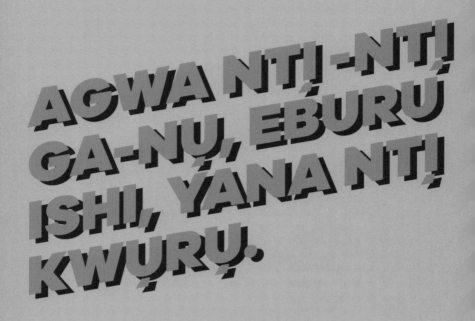

AGWA NTỊ-NTỊ GA-NỤ, EBURU ISHI, YANA NTỊ KWỤRỤ.

You can only warn someone so many times before you have to let life show them what you kept trying to protect them from. Some people are just damaged beyond your repair. It's important to snap out of trying to fix people like this; you'll find that it's like trying to use paint to fill a hole in the wall – it will never be enough. Remain compassionate but remember that it's not your responsibility to rescue anybody from their unresolved trauma. It's theirs.

translation
when you warn the ear, it doesn't listen, but when you cut the head the ear follows.

SURROUND YOURSELF WITH PEOPLE WHO HONOUR HOW YOU FEEL.

People who make you feel like you're 'too dramatic' or 'too emotional' are not the right people to surround yourself with because they will continually make you doubt your own instincts. This is dangerous because there is no voice you should listen to more than the voice of your own gut. A lot of the time, when people strangle our emotions, it's because they haven't yet learnt to face their own. It's important to understand that there ARE people in this world who will make room for you. People who will wait a little longer to understand you. Because you are worth it and they see it. Even if you can't find people like that, try to be that person for yourself.

SHOWING UP

The worst thing you can do is tell a friend in need of serious support 'I'm here if you need to talk to me', then suddenly flake on them or magically become busier than the bees in the sky just because you can't quite seem to face the 'burden' of being there for your friend. If you've never been on the receiving end of a flaky friendship, grab a tea and have a listen.

Understand that the word friend carries a bond, my friend. If you tell someone that you are going to be there for them and you flake on them, this is telling of your character. You run from anything that makes you look deeper at yourself. Think about it: in order to be there for someone who is going through an incredibly tough time emotionally, you have to also be able to relate to them and to relate to them, you have to put yourself in a position where you are as vulnerable as they are.

Equally, anybody who sees **you** in a state where you're so depressed that you're in need of serious intervention and does nothing was never your friend. If you were smart enough to make the choice to leave, congratulate yourself because you lost nothing. In fact, you gained an insight that can only be taught through experience: people who fail to show up for you at moments when you need them the most do not deserve to eat with you.

Not everybody is brave enough to even show up so appreciate the people who actually do.

At the same time, it is important to understand that people do have lives and their own problems but if people can find time to hang out with their mates, watch their favourite football matches and even tweet for hours on end, please know that they can make out time to speak to you if they want to but they just don't believe you are worthy of their time. And that's okay. We all make time for what we believe is necessary.

If people don't want to show up for you, kindly show them the door. This is your life. You are in charge.

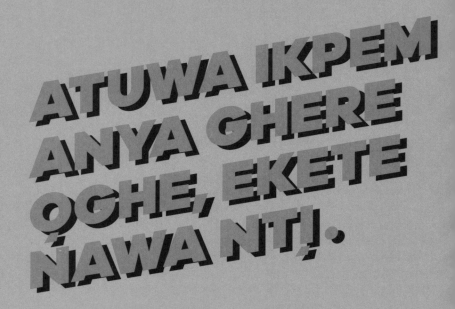

ATUWA IKPEM ANYA GHERE OGHE, EKETE ŃAWA NTỊ.

People will always find a way to notice with a message that nudges their conscience. It's not your job to make people feel better about themselves. It's not your job to silence your truth in fear of awakening someone else's insecurities. No matter what shape you twist your mouth in when you speak, someone will still feel attacked. Focus on your truth, focus on your message, focus on you. People will heal when they're ready.

translation
when you start talking about things with holes in them, the basket starts listening.

be
nice
to
people
for
no
reason.

But don't get attached to how you think they should react. Majority of the time, you're not going to get the exact reaction you had envisioned but let the happiness of another soul be your reward. Becoming angry at someone for not being 'as excited' as you wanted them to be only reveals that your intentions of being nice to them aren't pure, they're ego-driven. Being nice to other people also invites kindness into your life without your having to make the effort of looking for it.

Don't forget to congratulate your friends, no matter how well they are doing.

Sometimes knowing that someone is rooting for you is enough.

Give people their flowers while they can still smell them.

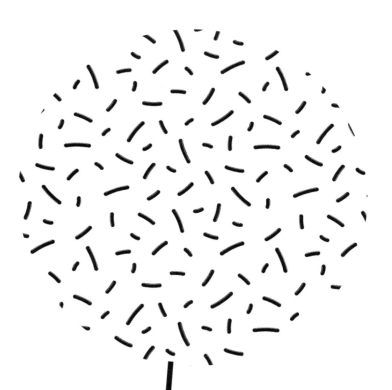

Take a moment to imagine a world where people actually appreciate the value you bring to that particular moment. Do you appreciate the value your friends bring to particular moments?

Love people while they're still here or learn to live without them.

HOLD ON TO THE FRIENDS WHO MAKE THE EFFORT TO

SAVE
YOUR
BIRTHDAY IN
THEIR
CALENDAR.

Repeat after me:

What's mine won't miss me.
What's mine won't miss me.
What's mine won't miss me.
What's mine won't miss me.
What's mine won't miss me.
What's mine won't miss me.
What's mine won't miss me.
What's mine won't miss me.
What's mine won't miss me.
What's mine won't miss me.
What's mine won't miss me.
What's mine won't miss me.
What's mine won't miss me.
What's mine won't miss me.
What's mine won't miss me.
What's mine won't miss me.
What's mine won't miss me.
What's mine won't miss me.
What's mine won't miss me.
What's mine won't miss me.

Everything meant for you is either here, or on its way. Life reaches a point where it suddenly becomes CRAZY difficult for literally no reason. You start losing everything: friends, opportunities, travel cards; the whole lot! You find yourself in a pit of despair, hanging up the decorations and sorting the invites for the 'WHY ME?!'-themed pity party you're about to throw yourself. Carrying a victim mentality is very addictive but we need to always remind ourselves that our blessings can never get lost on the way. Anything meant for us will work out, will stay, will make sense – regardless of what is happening around us. Missed out on an opportunity? If it was meant for you, it would have either worked out or re-aligned itself somehow. No sweat. Lost out on a friendship or relationship? If it was meant for the person you need to be, it would have worked out. No sweat. Life really doesn't require the amount of stress we exert on it most of the time. Learning to accept that everything is where it needs to be will give you the peace and clarity that you need to focus on what really matters: yourself. If you feel like you're trying too hard - especially with people, guess what? You probably are.

What's real cannot be forced.

YOU'LL MEAN THE WORLD TO SOMEONE ONE DAY.*

*And it won't just be your mum.

us. us.
us. us.
us. us.
us. us.
us. us.

us. us.
us. us.
us. us.
us. us.
us. us.

IT'S OKAY TO WANT TO BE LOVED.

Most people who claim that they don't care about love may be deliberately closing themselves off as a form of self-protection. This is totally understandable, especially if they've been hurt in the past.

But if you're someone who, deep down, wants to be loved, do not feel ashamed. We are all human beings. We want to feel valued, accepted and appreciated. This does not make us weak, needy or damaged. Its makes us wholesome, alive and in touch with our emotions. A lot of the time, we see the need to be loved in a negative light because we are in a generation of false self-sufficiency, quick bounce-backs and hidden feelings. But what we must understand is that people who hide their feelings are in a lot more pain than those who don't. It requires a lot of hurt and effort to silence yourself to the extent that you become used to feeling 'numb'. What a lot of people don't understand about being 'numb' is that the more you silence your sadness, the less happiness you will be experiencing because you are narrowing the range of emotions you are allowing yourself to feel. But the sooner you make peace with feelings that scare you, the more deeply you will experience happiness and other positive emotions because you will be making room for balance.

Love and pride are like oil and water. The two will never

If a person is withholding vulnerablity from you, it's sometimes because their pride is more important than forming a bond with you. Pride is the product of fear. The ego is terrified of being in a position of doubt. Pride offers protection. The ego sees vulnerability as a threat. But to love is to weaken the walls the ego has built and this is the ego's worst nightmare. If someone has more pride than vulnerability to show you, they are not in a position to properly love you.

Mixed signals aren't mysterious.

Mixed signals are the prelude to manipulation.

When it comes to dealing with people on a personal basis, I've learnt to take indecisive behaviour as a 'no'. In doing this, peace lasts longer for me. Having had to deal with so much disappointment in my life, I've developed an 'if you don't want me now, don't check for me later' policy. And it's working.

People know what they want; if they're indecisive, they ain't for you honey. If you're waiting for a person to make their mind up about you, this is life's push notification telling you it's time to work on your self-confidence. Big time. Stop waiting to be appreciated. If they can't see your value, let 'em stay blind!

Life's way too short and you are way too valuable to be waiting for people to give you permission to adore yourself. The most beautiful thing about progress is that it's never too late to start. People giving mixed signals love to remain unpredictable to keep you in a malleable position of dependency on them because it makes you and them both feel needed – a big fat ego stroke. This is not okay.

Once you snap out of the fear of being alone, you become invincible. Your life finally becomes yours to shape.

Empty promises are often a distraction. You complain that you're feeling disrespected. The other person paints your reaction as more damaging than the damage they have done to your self-esteem. You say that you are finally tired and are going to walk out and into a space that welcomes you. They panic. They promise you that 'it won't happen again' and that they'll 'change'. You know they won't change. You know it will happen again. But you silence your instincts for the nth time and you choose them over you. You betray your gut and you stay. Months pass while you wait for the promise of change. It never happens. How long do you intend to keep choosing other people over yourself? When will you learn that apologies are invalid without changed behaviour? What do you fear you will lose by ridding yourself of people who will always leave you hanging?

Kind-hearted people often fall for the idea of a sweet gesture before it even happens. Manipulative people capitalise on this trait and end up delivering more promises than actions. By the time you realise that you've been scammed with words, you're on your own with a pile of promises to overthink about.

EMPTY PROMISES ARE OFTEN A DISTRACTION.

Stop hanging out with people who talk over you in group conversations. They do not respect you.

Stop hanging out with people who love to dump their problems on you while making no room to listen to yours.

Stop hanging out with people who change the way they treat you when they're around people they want to suck up to.

Stop hanging out with people who only support you when it benefits them.

Stop hanging out with people who you show up for and support, but when it's your turn they have an excuse ready, every time.

Stop hanging out with people who also hang out with people who don't like you. As much as it's possible to be civil, it's near impossible to remain 'neutral' between enemies.

Stop hanging out with people who only invite you to events to make themselves look good.

Stop hanging out with people who conceal their friendship with you because of what their other friends may think.

Stop hanging out with people who only appear in your life to find out how they can better themselves, then disappear.

Stop hanging out with people who constantly go out of their way to hang out with people they swear they don't like.

Stop hanging out with people who think it's cool to trick other people. Manipulation of people's feelings isn't anything to be proud of.

Stop hanging out with people who keep flaking on you without making the effort to rearrange plans. They don't care about you or your time.

Stop hanging out with people who don't know how to be honest with themselves. They will never be honest with you either.

Stop hanging out with people who make you feel embarrassed about things you are passionate about.

Stop hanging out with people who love to talk you out of your ambitions but hide behind 'playing devil's advocate'.

Stop hanging out with people who ditch you when you are in a dark and lonely place mentally. They were never your friends to begin with.

Stop hanging out with people who make jokes out of your insecurities, then, when you feel offended, tell you that you can't 'take a joke'.

Stop hanging out with people who tell you of malicious things said about you behind your back but not what they said in response to them.

Ị TUO ONYE SHIRI IHE, Ọ SHIE ỌDỌ.

translation
when you praise the person who cooked, they will cook again.

My mother taught me: no matter how small the deed, always show gratitude. We are never too big to say 'thank you'. It's almost as though the obvious is being stated here but I'm pretty sure you will have come across people who just do not have any manners at all. It does not matter how close you are to someone; you are not entitled to another human being's kindness. When I come across people with poor manners, I have to assume that they have not been brought up very well, because the amount of effort you put into asking for a favour is the same amount you should put into showing gratitude. You ever come across people who never fail to give you an underwhelming response every time you make a massive effort for them? Aside from their being ungrateful, this is actually a control tactic of theirs to keep you on your feet. I'll explain further. We make large efforts for people we want to impress because we care about how they view us. Sometimes the people we choose to care about aren't good for us because they turn the care we have for them into a sociopathic game where they enjoy watching us work harder for their validation so they deliberately suppress any positive reactions to us.

If you ever find yourself in a situation like this, stop doing them favours, if you have that option. If you do not have that option (e.g. they are a family member), try your best to continue sharing your kindness but, from now on, stop internalising their reactions. They are not happy people and you cannot fix them with your kindness, no matter how hard you try.

If you feel like you've been that person being described, it is never too late to start being kinder to people. You need to try to understand why you are choosing to be horrible to people who are nice to you; what is it you are trying to protect yourself from? What has hurt you? How long will you allow this pain to dictate the way you choose to treat people who are kind to you? Chasing people away may have no effect at first, until you look around and realise that nobody is there anymore, all thanks to you. Try not to be that person.

EXPLAINING
WHY YOU
FEEL HURT IS
NOT ALWAYS
WORTH IT.

Good intentions, no matter how pure, are not guaranteed to be understood or received in the same spirit. The only two things in life we can control are our intentions and our reactions. Everything else happens as it needs to, whether it feels like it's occured in our favour or not.

No matter how pure your purpose, you will remain vulnerable to ingratitude, and reciprocation isn't guaranteed, nor is it mandatory. Underappreciation hurts, but not being able to explain the source of your pain hurts even more. Most of the time, we have difficulty expressing our feelings simply because we haven't given ourselves enough time to process them.

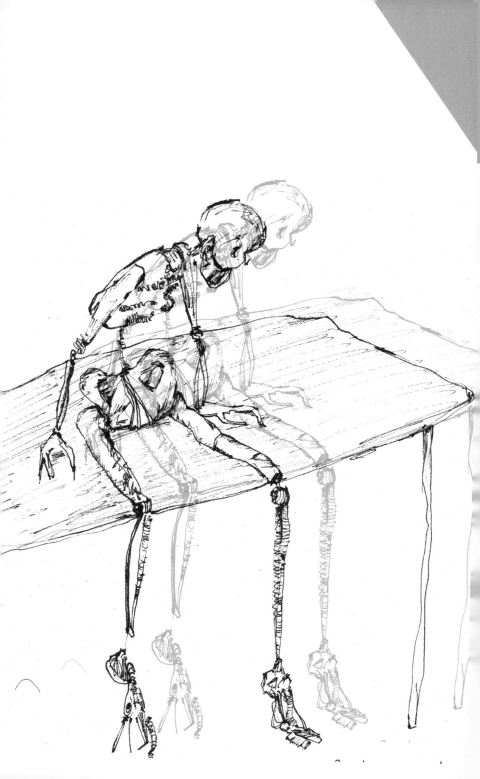

FORMING ATTACHMENTS TO EXPECTATIONS WILL ONLY CREATE DISAPPOINTMENT.

When you love a person, detach yourself from your expectations of how they 'should' react to your affection and focus instead on what this feeling means to YOU. All the people we love will eventually disappoint us. But if we learn to manage our expectations and become detached from the unrealistic idea of people living up to them, we will discover that if we can learn to control your expectations, we can control our reality.

May you find comfort in your identity instead of seeking safety in other people's. May you learn to visit other people's worlds without feeling compelled to build a home in them.

Lower your expectations of others.

Raise your expectations of yourself.

NWA SỊ NA NNEYE AGAHỤ ARAHA ỤRA, AGAHỤ ARAHA KEYE.

A crying baby must remain awake all night to keep their mother awake all night. Anybody who wastes your time is also wasting their own time in the process, whether they believe they are gaining from it or not. In the long run, selfish behaviour is never rewarded. Nothing we do goes unnoticed in this cause-and-effect world we live in. Whether you believe it or not, what you choose to do always comes back to you in some way or another in the end.

translation
the child that says their
mother will not sleep, will
also not sleep.

**YOU DESERVE
BETTER.**

FEELING FORGOTTEN?

It's the worst. You feel invisible. You feel like all your efforts to make your mark will just never be enough. You wonder what it is that makes you so easy to be forgotten. You try to be bolder, louder, brighter, funnier. Nothing lasts. No one laughs. You beat yourself up. You isolate yourself because what's the point in being around people who can't tell the difference between your presence and your absence?

But what you must realise is that you are not here to entertain anybody. You are everything you need to be for you. As long as you aren't being a total prick or harming anyone (including yourself), there isn't a 'wrong' way to be you. If you're around people who make you feel easily forgotten, you're around the wrong people. If you are physically unable to get away from them because of elements out of your control, don't forget that your mind can take you anywhere you yearn to be. Become your source of peace. Become your source of entertainment. Find something that keeps you alive and get lost in it. Try not to let that thing be a person, because getting lost in a person only strays you further away from the person you will always need the most:

Ọ CHOGA MGBALAGA SỊ A RUỌLA YA ANYA.

If someone seems to have a problem with you, it's merely an extension of their underlying problem with their own self. Yes, it's possible to be a problem in someone's life ... but you aren't the problem here. People like this will often gaslight you into believing everything is your fault by painting your reaction to their toxic behaviour as worse than their behaviour. You owe yourself peace. Rather than dwelling on what didn't work out, it's time to make room for the greatness on its way into your life.

translation
when someone is looking
for an excuse to escape,
they'll blame anything.

TRY NOT
TO SHARE
YOURSELF WITH
PEOPLE WHO
DON'T WANT
TO MAKE ROOM
FOR

YOU.

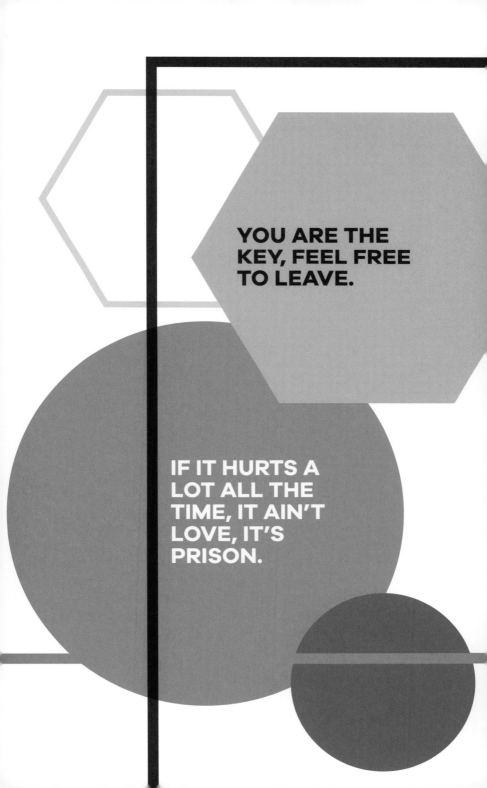

YOU ARE THE KEY, FEEL FREE TO LEAVE.

IF IT HURTS A LOT ALL THE TIME, IT AIN'T LOVE, IT'S PRISON.

EZIGBO ỤKA NA ESHI ṄA UDE NMAYA NA-APỤTA.

Drunk feelings are real. Drunk texts and phone calls should be taken with a pinch of salt but are still worth making an effort to understand, because even if they are exaggerated or false, they still reveal something of the way the drunk person feels about their self. No matter what state we are in, we will always project onto others the way we feel about ourselves.

Yes, it is possible to evoke a feeling in someone else which means they reach out to you, but in the end, nothing anybody ever does is completely because of you. For example, if an emotionally abusive ex drunk-contacts you out of the blue, this is not because they have suddenly unlearnt their toxic behaviour and made the necessary efforts to repair their self esteem overnight. Building the self-esteem necessary to unlearn toxic behaviour is something that will require a prolonged period of self-isolation to overcome deep-rooted traumas that have created these harmful behavioural patterns in the first place. Unlearning is not a late-night drunk revelation.

As flattering as they may feel, drunk texts are barely a romantic gesture if they are coming from a toxic space.

translation
out of the wine, comes
the truth.

CERTAIN MISTAKES MUST NEED TO BE MADE, IN ORDER FOR THE REAL GROWTH TO BEGIN.

Mistakes exist to show you loopholes in your own behavioural patterns. Without making mistakes, you'll never have any perspective, character or experience.

No matter how embarrassed you are by your mistakes, ultimately what matters is how much you learn about yourself from them – not how quickly.

If you made a mistake at the expense of someone else, it does not matter whether or not you have learnt your lesson: you are not entitled to anybody's forgiveness. But even if you cannot make amends with that person directly, all is not lost. Just treat the next person better.

It's better to make valuable mistakes than to miss out on life by playing it safe.

You are allowed to outgrow people. And people are allowed to outgrow you. Often we find ourselves getting way too invested in and attached to particular friendships. But it's so understandable, especially when you've grown up with that person or been through so much with them. It's hard to imagine a life without them. But life happens regardless of what we want. We cannot expect the people we love to move at our pace. And we can't expect the same from them either. It just isn't fair. People grow, their priorities change with their opinions and, before you know it, they just might not have time for you anymore. We've all, at some point, been guilty of throwing a tantrum when our cherished friend can no longer hang out with us, but learning to let go of what no longer serves us is the key.

IT IS VERY OKAY TO CHANGE YOUR MIND ABOUT PEOPLE.

'I forgive you but I've changed my mind about you' is a totally valid stance.

Take your time. True forgiveness of others doesn't happen until you have been able sit still with yourself, unpack your own reasoning and finally let go of the judgement you've been placing not just on others, but on yourself.

Accepting that you have let yourself down despite all the efforts you've made to maintain the standards you expect for yourself makes you feel like a fraud. It's nobody's place to rush you or or pressure you into forgiving anybody for anything, no matter how much the sentiment benefits you in the moment. Forgiveness of yourself can take a lifetime.

Even if you accept an apology in the heat of the moment, only later returning to your senses, you are allowed to change your mind.

ACCEPTED APOLOGIES
ARE NOT CONTRACTS.

REGRET
WORSE
REJECT

Moments of realisation are often followed by moments of regret. But use that regret to guide you through to becoming a better you. It's better to hear a 'no' than to wonder for the rest of your life what could have existed on the other side of that moment. Uncertainties haunt us forever when we know there was always a chance. Certainty is clarity.

IS
THAN
ON.

You'll get over it. When it comes to healing, take as LONG as you need to get over it. To grow past it. To no longer let it have power over you. Thanks to social media, there's this overwhelming pressure to look like you've moved on quickly; there's almost this unspoken competition that whoever cares less wins. Ignore it. Be as fragile as you need to be. Stop looking at their profile. Block them. Mute them. Even when you feel tempted to still have a snoop, remind yourself that you are searching for validation in the wrong place.

The process of 'getting over it' is tough because it involves unlearning habits and weaning yourself off an environment you are familiar with. You must understand that this is not easy for ANYONE. A lot of the time, what looks like someone else moving on quickly is actually just a bunch of vital emotions shoved away in a mental attic. Some people are really good at running away from their feelings. But the thing about running away from your feelings is that you are actually running in a very large circle ... you will eventually get back to where you started. Your feelings will eventually hit you. If you're running, you are only kidding yourself.

Learning to process every emotion for as long as your body needs to is the only way to heal. Honesty with self is the best gift you can reward yourself with. Because being in denial only harms you further in the long run. Don't be ashamed if you feel like it's taken you longer than it 'should' to appear to have 'gotten over it'. Our emotions have no expiry date. They will stay with us until they have served their purpose in our lives.

Comparing your healing time to someone else's will only prolong your healing. We all have different pain thresholds. Some of us are also better at hiding the way we feel than others. But we are all human and we all bleed, cry and piss the same stuff.

There's no shame in pain. Feel it all and remind yourself that whatever it is that you are feeling right now – be it happiness, sadness or even boredom – is temporary and will pass like the seasons do. You've got this. Keep your head up, stay strong. It'll get better soon.

IKE ANAHỤ AGBAGO AGBAGO, ỌNA AGBADA ÁGBADA.

translation
physical strength never remains permanent. it must eventually decline.

You won't be the 'it' thing forever.

Instagram might shut down one day and suddenly nobody will care about your 80,000 followers.

Relevance in the offline world is key. Having online value and being able to monetise it is an excellent skill for right now, but what about having great character, something social media can never show?

Being idolised and borderline worshipped online can have a negative mental effect, making people feel entitled, selfish and above judgement and critcism. This sort of mental state can negatively influence the way people behave towards themselves and others offline.

Having talent, especially online talent, does not automatically make you a 'nice' person. Some famous Hollywood actors may be beating their wives. Certain 'artists' may be hiding under the guise of artistic expression to lure women into being sexually abused.

It's nice to be admired, but what's most important is how other people feel while they're in your company. Are you a listener? Do you make room for other people? Do you make the effort to be kind without expecting anything back?

When you die, your tombstone isn't going to say how many followers you had on Instagram (unless you request that). Your tombstone will commemorate the energy you left behind.

remember

why

you

left.

FEELING SECURE IN YOUR SOLITUDE

Being insecure and feeling 'lonely' is the ultimate recipe for self-destruction. You've got to teach yourself to feel secure in your solitude. Boredom is the ideal breeding ground for bad decisions. Occupy yourself with your goals. Honestly. Boredom and insecurity are the perfect combination for a lot of poor choices.

The more you love yourself, the better the decisions that you make. When you focus on making your life as interesting and fulfilling as possible for yourself, you organically outgrow your old troubled self.

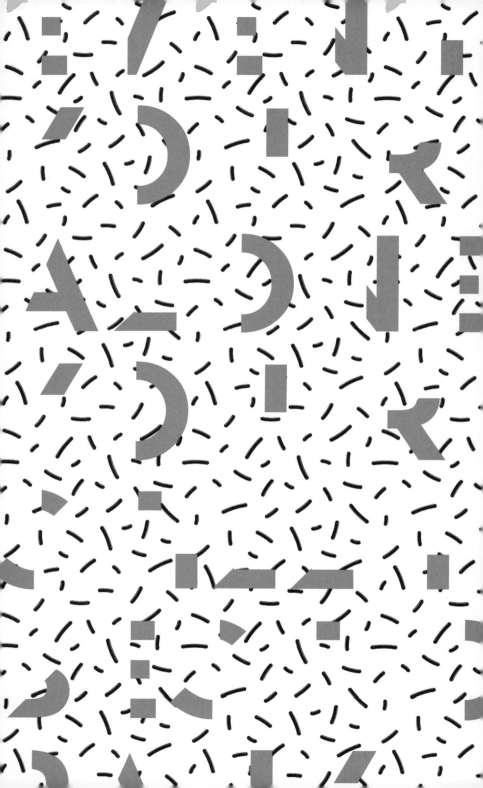

Even if you're alone, you're still in the best company. **Being alone will always be a win because you already live a full and amazing life on your own, with great prospects and a delightful future.**

This book is dedicated to oiling your skin, taking your vitamins, going to cool places alone once in a while and avoiding scenarios that make you second-guess yourself – no matter how intense the dopamine rush is.

May you find security in your solitude.

Chidera Eggerue, popularly known as the Slumflower, is an award-winning blogger, speaker, creative director and a presenter of the The MOBO Awards. Her blog The Slumflower – a name inspired by the streets of her native Peckham in South London – addresses the subjects of female empowerment, self-confidence, self-love, black hair, fashion and self-exploration. Chidera was recently the only British girl to make it on to BuzzFeed's '30 Black Girls You Should Follow on Instagram' list. She has featured on Women's Hour and ITV News as well as in *i-D*, *Elle*, *Fader*, *InStyle*, the *Evening Standard*, the *Daily Mail* and *Stylist*.